Celebrate Creation
(Grades 1–3)

Written by Sandie E. Dusa

Illustrated by Don O'Connor

Cover Illustrated by Kathryn Marlin

All rights reserved—Printed in the U.S.A.
Copyright © 2000 Shining Star Publications
A Division of Frank Schaffer Publications, Inc.
23740 Hawthorne Blvd., Torrance, CA 90505

Unless otherwise indicated, the New International Version of the Bible was used in preparing the activities in this book. Scripture taken from the HOLY BIBLE, NEW INTERNATIONAL VERSION. Copyright © 1973, 1978, 1984 International Bible Society. Used by permission of Zondervan Bible Publishers.

Table of Contents

To Parents and Teachers

What a fun way for children to learn all about creation! *Celebrate Creation* is filled with a wonderful variety of activities children can do to learn about the many gifts God created for us. Children will work puzzles, solve riddles, do research, perform finger plays, write poems, make crafts, create murals, and draw pictures, among many other things.

Each day of creation is featured in its own chapter and includes Bible verses, questions for discussion, and fantastic facts, as well as activities designed to stimulate children's interest in the incredible power of God. Some pages are addressed to the teacher and may require adult supervision and preparation. Others have been designed specifically for children to complete. Regardless of the format, each activity features easy-to-follow directions and will keep children motivated and interested.

You will love watching children have fun as they learn all about the beautiful things God created and gave to us to enjoy!

Day and Night
Based on Genesis 1:1–5

When Kids Ask . . .

Children love the story of creation. They can hear it over and over again and still have a lot of questions concerning many aspects of it.

Below are some commonly asked questions about God and creation. Next to them are Bible passages that will help answer the questions. You can use the questions in several ways. One way is to give each question to a child and have him or her pose the question to you out loud. Find and read the answers in the Bible and discuss them with the children. Or, divide the children into groups. Give each group a question and have it come up with an answer. You can either give the groups the Bible references or read them together after the children come up with their own answers.

1. *How old is God? When was He born?* (Revelation 1:8)

2. *What did earth look like in the beginning?* (Genesis 1:2)

3. *How did God make things?* (Genesis 1:3; Psalm 29:3a, 4, 7, 8, 9—God spoke things into being every day of creation.)

4. *Where does darkness come from?* (Job 38:19–20—God has homes for darkness and light. Both darkness and light are necessary to God's eternal plan; Matthew 27:45—The Creator used darkness to speak to the world on the day His Son was crucified. For three hours, darkness fell on the land.)

5. *Does all light come from the sun?* (Psalm 104:2—No. God separated the darkness from the light before He created the sun. God, Himself, is robed in light; John 8:12)

Fantastic Facts

Below are some fascinating facts relating to light and dark. Put these on a bulletin board and let the children add to them, illustrate them, or write about them in journals. Or, let groups of children choose one to prepare a report on, create a mural for, find a Bible verse that relates to it, etc.

- The eyes of a starfish, located at the tip of each arm, can only detect light or dark.

- One variety of shrimp does not have any eyes since it thrives in pitch black waters.

- There are some creatures living in the darkest part of the ocean whose bodies have built-in flashlights.

- Light travels at a distance of 186,282 miles per second.

- Ultraviolet light is invisible to human eyes. It is both productive and harmful. It can burn the skin and cause skin and eye damage. It is useful for destroying bacteria and sterilizing medical equipment.

- When electricity jumps from a cloud, it makes lightning.

- The time from a lightning flash to a clap of thunder tells how far away a storm is. Usually, each second represents about $\frac{1}{5}$ of a mile.

Matching Block Designs

Based on Genesis 1:1–5

And God said, "Let there be light," and there was light. God saw that the light was good, and he separated the light from the darkness. (Genesis 1:3–4)

God had a purpose for everything He created. God created the earth and everything in it for His pleasure and your enjoyment. There is usefulness in both light and darkness. Tell the children to look around. Ask where they see designs of dark and light. Then prepare the game below for the children to play.

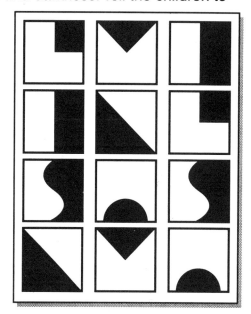

Materials Needed:

a large sheet of posterboard, two enlarged copies of the block patterns below, glue, two buttons

Directions:

Glue the blocks onto a large sheet of posterboard in four rows of three blocks each. Make sure the blocks are identically positioned (not reversed) for identical matching.

To Play:

A player has two turns to throw buttons onto two matching blocks. Before a turn can be taken, the player must tell something God created that is "dark" or "light." (Scoring is optional.)

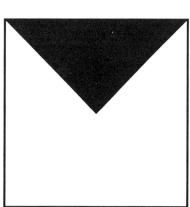

SS48836

The Earth's Beginning

Based on Genesis 1:1–5

In the beginning God created the heavens and the earth. (Genesis 1:1)

The Bible tells us that the earth was formless and empty. It was dark, and it had _____.

To find out the answer, follow the paths. Write the first letter of each picture in the empty boxes.

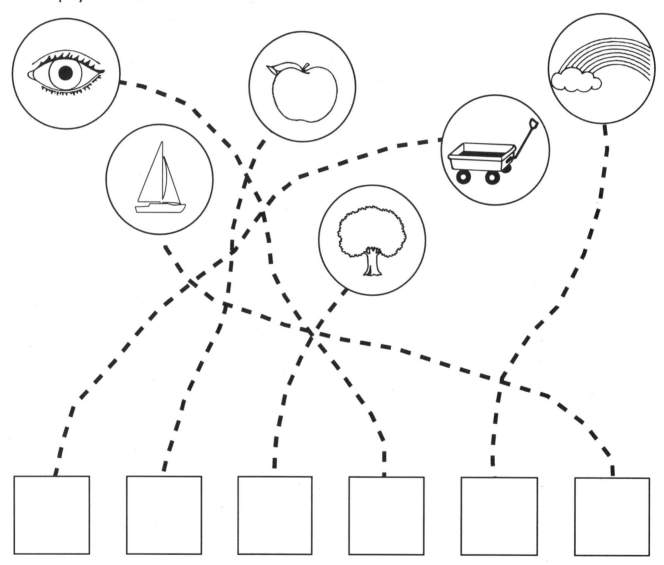

For More Fun

Write the names of three bodies of water you know. They can be lakes, rivers, or oceans.

_____ _____ _____

"Let There Be Light!"

Based on Genesis 1:1–5

And God said, "Let there be light," and there was light. God saw that the light was good, and he separated the light from the darkness. God called the light "day," and the darkness he called "night." And there was evening, and there was morning—the first day. (Genesis 1:3–5)

God gave us light so that we can see the many beautiful things He created. Follow the directions below to create your very own light out of darkness.

Materials Needed:

8 ½" x 11" sheet of white paper, black crayon, copy of poem below, glue, coin

Directions:

1. Cut out and glue the poem to the center of the paper.

2. Color all around the poem using the black crayon. Rub hard so that the whole page is heavily coated with black crayon.

3. Use the coin to scrape a design in the black crayon and to let the "light" shine through the "dark."

4. Memorize the poem and say it to a friend.

Day and Night

Out of black,

Came the light.

God made day.

God made night.

Darkness and Light Box

Based on Genesis 1:1–5

Ask the children how they feel when they are in the dark. What makes darkness go away? Where does darkness come from? Where does light come from? Is darkness good or bad? When?

Read Genesis 1:1–5 to the children. Explain that before the earth was made, there was nothing but deep, black waters. God had a plan in His mind. He said, "Let there be light," and light appeared. God separated the darkness from the light because they each were necessary. He called the light "day" and the darkness "night."

Make the box below to let the children experience firsthand the light coming out of the darkness.

Materials Needed:

one 12" x 12" x 12" cardboard box (or larger)
packing or other strong tape
black felt
glue gun
scissors or knife
flashlight
black electrical tape

Directions:

1. Tape all seams of the box to seal off any incoming light.

2. Cut a viewing hole in the front of the box.

3. Use a glue gun to attach black felt around the edges of the hole to form a light barrier.

4. Attach a flashlight to the side of the box by cutting a hole and inserting the head of the flashlight securely. (Black electrical tape on the inside and outside of the box will hold the flashlight in place.)

5. Make sure the "on/off" switch on the flashlight is positioned for the children to use easily.

6. Let the children take turns using the box. They may recite *And God said, "Let there be light"* as they operate the flashlight.

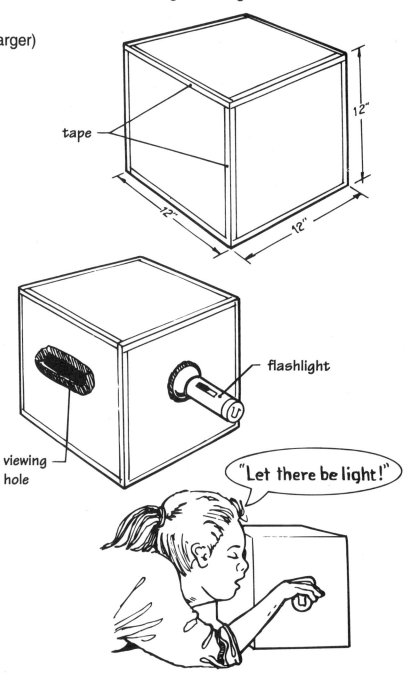

First Day Fun

Based on Genesis 1:1–5

So much happened on the first day of creation! To learn about that first day, circle one letter in each block to form a word in each row going across. Write your answers on the numbered blanks below. The words in the word box will help you. But be careful—only five of the eight words are in the blocks.

N	A	P	G	Y
E	M	O	T	S

T	A	T	R	H
W	E	R	E	R

F	I	T	H	K
L	P	G	S	T

E	N	M	T	Y
R	A	R	M	H

W	A	G	S	T
N	I	E	H	R

WORD BOX

FIRST	WATER	THERE
LIGHT	EMPTY	MAKER
EARTH	NIGHT	

1. _____   2. _____

3. _____   4. _____

5. _____

SS48836

Water and Sky
Based on Genesis 1:6–8

When Kids Ask . . .

Below are some questions the children may ask in regards to the second day of creation. Give four children one of the questions to ask, or divide the children into groups and give each group a question. You can use the Bible verses listed to help you answer the questions, or you can let the children come up with their own answers.

1. *What is the sky?* (Genesis 1:6–8—*Expanse,* a wide infinite area of atmospheric space, is difficult to define in unscientific terms. Children may more easily grasp the meaning of "waters above" and "waters below" to reach an understanding of the "sky" in between.)

2. *What are the "waters above?"* (Job 36:27; Jeremiah 10:12–13; Psalm 148:4; Explain to the children how rain, snow, sleet, etc., all come from the sky.)

3. *What are the "waters below?"* (Psalm 33:7; Job 38:16)

4. *Does God live in the sky?* (Deuteronomy 33:26—God's home is in heaven which is above the skies as we see them; 2 Samuel 22:10–12)

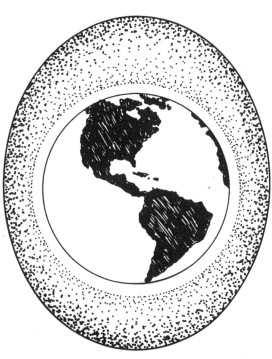

Fantastic Facts

Below are some fascinating facts relating to water and sky. Put these on a bulletin board and let the children add to them, illustrate them, or write about them in journals. Or, let groups of children choose one to prepare a report on, create a mural for, find a Bible verse that relates to it, etc.

- Two gases make up the earth's atmosphere—nitrogen and oxygen. This atmosphere protects people from dangerous things like ultraviolet light and harmful particles and debris.

- The ozone layer, miles above the earth, screens out dangerous ultraviolet rays and protects life on earth.

- Earth is the only planet in the solar system which contains oxygen and liquid water in its environment to sustain life.

- More than 70% of earth's surface is water.

Wonderful Water Cycle

Based on Genesis 1:6–8

Read Genesis 1:6–8 to the children. Define *expanse.* Invite the children to tell what they know about water, how they use it, etc. Ask them where water comes from. How is water used? What would happen if there was no water? Next, encourage the children to describe the sky. What do they think it is made from? Can they touch it or hold it? What keeps the sky up? Ask the children if they can divide water. Tell them that God designed waters to collect above the sky and below the sky. He did this in order to make the earth a healthy, beautiful place for us to live.

Help the children learn about the water cycle. Give each child a copy of the pictures and sentence strips below. Have the children cut them apart, number them, and glue each sentence strip and corresponding picture to its own sheet of paper. The children can color the pictures and staple their pages together to create their very own water cycle books.

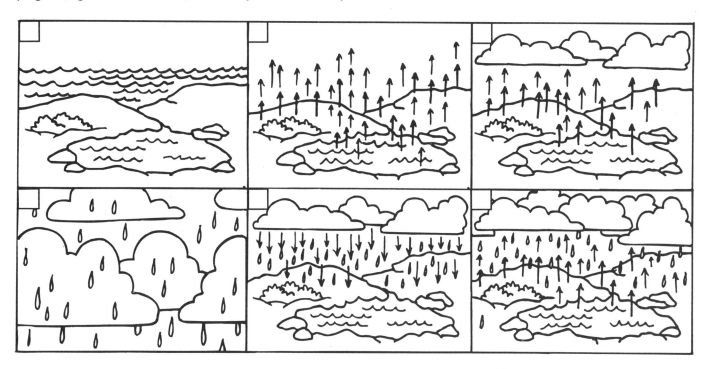

1. Water is everywhere on the land and in the sea.

2. Water changes into vapor and rises up into the sky.

3. The vapor in the sky makes clouds when it turns into water droplets.

4. The droplets fall from the sky as rain.

5. The rain falls into the sea and on the ground.

6. Some of the water rises back up into the sky to make more clouds.

Creation Bingo

Based on Genesis 1:6–8

Read Genesis 1:6–8 to the children. Ask them what forms of water they can name that come down from the sky. Then read the following scriptures to the children: Psalm 148:4, 8; Job 37:16; Job 38:22–30, 37. Have the children write or draw each form of water they hear on a sheet of paper.

To play Creation Bingo, make one copy of the game board below for each child. Depending on the age levels of the children, fill in the blank boxes with letters A–Z or numbers 1–10 or 1–100. Make each card different. (Some children may fill in their own cards before play begins.) Play the game in the same manner as BINGO. For example, you might call out "Cloud–M" or "Wind–7," etc. Dried kidney beans or cereal pieces make suitable markers.

cloud	rain	snow	wind	fog

Water and Sky Wordsearch

Based on Genesis 1:6–8

Day 2

Think of the many things you do each day that involve the sky or water. What wonderful gifts God gave us!

The words listed below all relate to the sky and water that God created on the second day. Find these 14 words in the wordsearch. Some are backwards, and some are upside down.

AIR	CLOUD	DEW	DROP	EARTH	FROZEN	HAIL
RAIN	SKY	SLEET	SNOW	STORM	WATER	WIND

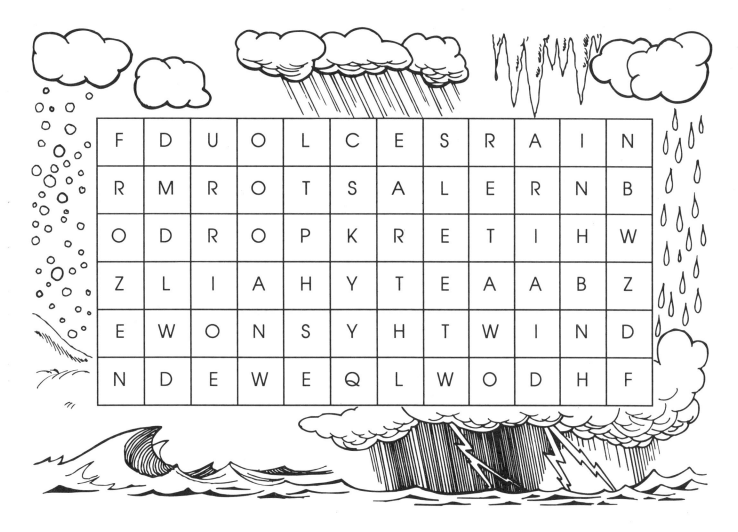

F	D	U	O	L	C	E	S	R	A	I	N
R	M	R	O	T	S	A	L	E	R	N	B
O	D	R	O	P	K	R	E	T	I	H	W
Z	L	I	A	H	Y	T	E	A	A	B	Z
E	W	O	N	S	Y	H	T	W	I	N	D
N	D	E	W	E	Q	L	W	O	D	H	F

For More Fun

Write two words that rhyme with *sky*. _____ _____

Write two words that rhyme with *snow*. _____ _____

SS48836

Fun With Air and Water

Based on Genesis 1:6–8

And God said, "Let there be an expanse between the waters to separate water from water." (Genesis 1:6)

God can do anything He wants to do. He created the sky to separate the waters above from the waters below.

To better understand this concept, try the experiment below.

Materials Needed:
clear plastic tumbler, medium-sized bowl, water, paper towels

Directions:

1. Fill the bowl with water.

2. Put the tumbler in the water and slowly turn it upside down.

3. Observe the water filling up the tumbler.

4. Lift the glass of water slowly. Watch how the water stays inside until the rim of the glass clears the surface of the water.

5. Write the names of two kinds of water above the sky.

   _____   _____

6. Write the names of two kinds of water below the sky.

   _____   _____

Land, Seas, Plants, Trees

Based on Genesis 1:9–13

Day 3

When Kids Ask . . .

Below are some questions the children may ask in regards to the third day of creation. Give five children one of the questions to ask, or divide the children into groups and give each group a question. You can use the Bible verses listed to help you answer the questions, or you can let the children come up with their own answers.

1. *What is "dry land?"* (Genesis 1:10—Note: It would be helpful to display a map or globe and point out the seven continents. Explain that the dry "land" is made up of mountains, hills, plains, etc. The waters were then gathered into oceans or seas.)

2. *Did God put gold in the earth?* (Job 28:5–6—Yes. Inside the earth are minerals and gems.)

3. *Why did God make rocks?* (Job 28:2—Rocks contain ores and minerals; Luke 19:40—Even rocks give glory to the Creator. Jesus told the Pharisees that even the rocks knew who He was and could cry out and give Him glory.)

4. *Can God see the inside of the earth?* (Psalm 95:4—Yes; Job 28:10—God sees where treasures are hiding. He helps men discover them.)

5. *Why did God make so many kinds of trees and plants?* (Psalm 96:12—God made all things to bring Him glory. The rocks and trees sing for the Lord; Genesis 1:29—The trees and plants were God's gift of food to animals and man; 1 Kings 10:12—Many plants and trees, like aloe, myrrh, and figs, are medicinal. Others are used for buildings, furniture, or musical instruments, such as the almugwood tree.)

Fantastic Facts

Below are some fascinating facts relating to land, seas, plants, and trees. Put these on a bulletin board and let the children add to them, illustrate them, or write about them in journals. Or, let groups of children choose one to prepare a report on, create a mural for, find a Bible verse that relates to it, etc.

- The crust (shell) of the earth is made of rock that varies from 5 to 20 miles thick.
- The temperature in the earth's core is above 1700 degrees Fahrenheit.
- Diamonds are the hardest natural substance and can cut through anything.
- Paint and dye colors are made from rock pigments crushed to powder.
- Coal is one of earth's greatest sources of fuel and energy. Plant materials, buried for years under pressure and heat, form coal.
- A saguaro cactus, 20 feet tall, can store 100 gallons of water in a 4-month period.
- Many cacti are excellent for eating. Prickly pear cacti are fed to cattle in Texas.
- The redwood tree is thought to be the tallest tree in the world. One is reported to be about 385 feet high.
- Some redwoods are the oldest living things—more than 3500 years old.
- Many drugs and medications for treating humans and animals are made from plant and animal poisons.

Dry Ground—Land

Based on Genesis 1:9–13

". . . let dry ground appear." And it was so. God called the dry ground "land" . . . (Genesis 1:9–10)

God gave us a lot of land to use for many, many things. The earth God created has seven continents. Look at a world map or globe and locate the seven continents.

The names of all seven continents appear in the puzzle below, but the vowels in each word are missing. Use the words in the word box to help you spell the names correctly. Fill in the missing vowels. Note: Two continents share a letter.

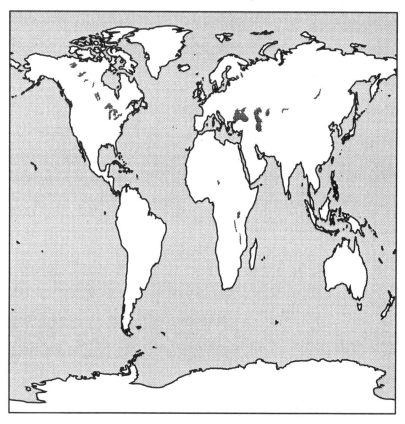

WORD BOX
AFRICA
ANTARCTICA
ASIA
AUSTRALIA
EUROPE
NORTH AMERICA
SOUTH AMERICA

S			T	H		M		R		C		■
	R		P			F	R		C			■
	N	T		R	C	T		C		S		
N		R	T	H		M		R		C		■
■			S	T	R			L		■	■	■

A Lot of Land

Based on Genesis 1:9–13

When God created land, He put mountains and valleys and hills and plains on it. What is the land like where you live? Draw two pictures. In the top box, draw a picture of what the land where you live looks like. In the bottom box, draw a picture of what you wish the land where you live looks like.

Seas of the Bible

Based on Genesis 1:9–13

. . . and the gathered waters he called "seas." And God saw that it was good. (Genesis 1:10)

God created many seas for us to enjoy. Look at the maps in the back of your Bible to find the bodies of water listed below. Put a check next to each one you find. Then fit them into the puzzle. One is done for you.

ADRIATIC (SEA)   AEGEAN (SEA)   BLACK (SEA)

CASPIAN (SEA)   GALILEE (SEA OF)   GREAT (SEA)

IONIAN (SEA)   RED (SEA)   SALT (SEA)

Perfectly Great Plants

Based on Genesis 1:9–13

Then God said, "Let the land produce vegetation: seed-bearing plants and trees on the land that bear fruit with seed in it, according to their various kinds." And it was so. The land produced vegetation: plants bearing seed according to their kinds and trees bearing fruit with seed in it according to their kinds . . . (Genesis 1:11–12)

Plants are vital to all people and all living creatures. They provide us with the air we breathe, food we eat, shade we sit in, and so much more! Let the children try the activities below with your guidance to better understand plants, their parts, and their uses.

Materials Needed:

a variety of fruits and vegetables; knife; magnifying glass; paper towels; pre-soaked, large lima beans; clear plastic cups; magazines; crayons or markers; construction paper; scissors; glue

Activity 1

Cut open the fruits and vegetables. Let the children observe the size, color, shape, and texture of each. Explain to the children that God made every seed with an outer coating and an inner food supply to help it begin a new plant of its own kind. Then let the children sort the seeds, wash them, and lay them out to dry. The children can use the dried seeds in collages.

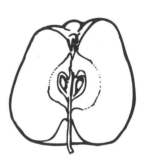

Activity 2

Pass a water-soaked lima bean to each child. Tell the children to notice the wrinkled seed coat. The children can use a magnifying glass to find a spot where the seed may be probed apart. Tell them to look for a tiny new plant with a tiny pair of leaves inside.

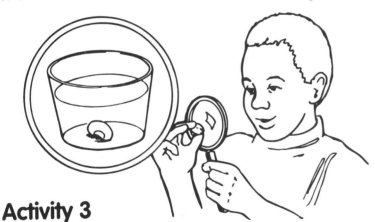

Activity 3

Have the children name fruit-bearing trees; vegetables containing seeds that we eat; fruits we eat after removing the seeds; etc. Let pairs of children cut out or draw pictures of fruits and vegetables they can use to create their own collages of fruits and vegetables that they categorize as they wish. You could give the pairs a predetermined number of categories they must have, or you could even give them the categories themselves. (Suggestions of categories—color, how grown, how eaten, when ripe, size, shape, etc.)

Seed Pictures

Based on Genesis 1:9–13

Seeds fascinate children! All of the plants God created start as tiny seeds. Let the children try some of the activities below to learn all about seeds.

Materials Needed:

pictures of plants and trees; dried seeds and beans; colorful sheets of posterboard, cut into 6" x 8" pieces; pencils; white glue (paste will not work); wooden craft sticks to use to apply glue

Directions:

Display pictures of plants and trees for the children to view. Then give each child a sheet of posterboard and a pencil. Have the children draw an outline of a plant or tree on their posterboard. (Encourage the children to make their drawings large so that they fill up most of the area of posterboard with their plant or tree outline.) Demonstrate how to apply glue with a craft stick and lay seeds right on and inside the lines. Be sure to apply glue to one small area at a time, about the size of a quarter, since the glue will dry quickly.

For More Fun

- Have one or two larger group pictures for children to work on together.

- Give each child a packet of seeds. Have the children glue the seeds into the shape of the plant the seeds grow into.

- Give each child a seed. Tell the children what their seeds grow into. Have them paste their seeds onto a sheet of paper, draw the plant it could one day grow into, and write a simple poem about it. Examples:

This little seed
Will one day be
A great big oak
With shade for me.

Though now I'm small,
One day you'll see,
Lots of green needles
On me—a pine tree!

Sun, Moon, and Stars

Based on Genesis 1:14–19

When Kids Ask . . .

Below are some questions the children may ask in regards to the fourth day of creation. Give each child one of the questions to ask, or divide the children into groups and give each group one or two questions. You can use the Bible verses listed to help you answer the questions, or you can let the children come up with their own answers.

1. *Why did God make the sun so bright?* (Genesis 1:14–15)

2. *Can God change the sun's light?* (Matthew 27:45–46—When Jesus was crucified, God made the sun stop shining. Darkness was on the earth for three hours; Joel 2:31—There will be another time when the sun turns to darkness. It will happen just before the day of the Lord.)

3. *Does the sun move?* (Ecclesiastes 1:5—Yes.)

4. *Where does the sun come from?* (Psalm 19:4–6—Heaven)

5. *Can God make the sun stand still?* (Joshua 10:13—Yes. God heard Joshua's prayer and helped his army win a battle.)

6. *Why did God make the moon?* (Psalm 104:19—It marks off the seasons; 1 Samuel 20:5—Some farmers plant and harvest their crops according to the moon's phases. The Israelites celebrated many feasts at New Moon festivals.)

7. *Does God know how many stars are in the sky?* (Psalm 147:4—Yes; Isaiah 40:26—Our powerful God even names each star. And not one of them gets lost. When you see a star fall, do you know where it goes? God does.)

8. *Is it wrong to worship the sun, moon, and stars?* (Deuteronomy 4:19—Yes.)

Fantastic Facts

Below are some fascinating facts relating to the sun, moon, and stars. Put these on a bulletin board and let the children add to them, illustrate them, or write about them in journals. Or, let groups of children choose one to prepare a report on, create a mural for, find a Bible verse that relates to it, etc.

• Some sections of the sun reach temperatures of 27 million degrees Fahrenheit.

• The diameter of the sun is 865,000 miles. That is 110 times that of earth.

• Stars make sounds which astronomers refer to as radio sources.

• The gravity of the sun and the moon produce the earth's tides.

• The moon orbits the earth approximately every 27 days.

• The sun is made up of gases—hydrogen and helium.

• The first human being to walk on the moon was Neil Armstrong, on July 20, 1969.

• The moon is $^1/_4$ the size of the earth.

• The sun is earth's nearest star.

Star Cookies

Based on Genesis 1:14–19

God made two great lights—the greater light to govern the day and the lesser light to govern the night. He also made the stars. (Genesis 1:16)

Discuss with the children why God made stars (they give light and heat; they provide navigational direction to ship captains, pilots, and astronauts; they helped the wise men find baby Jesus—Matthew 2:2). Then tell them a little bit about stars. (For example, the sun is a star. It is about 100 times larger than the earth. Other stars look small because they are far, far away. Stars don't really twinkle, but their light travels through the atmosphere and makes them appear to twinkle. The Milky Way galaxy is made up of millions and millions of stars. Scriptures tell us that God put every star in place—Psalm 8:3; God counts the stars, and each one has a name—Psalm 147:4; no two stars are alike. They differ in size, color, and beauty—1 Corinthians 15:41; Jesus is called the "bright Morning Star"—Revelation 22:16.)

Then let the children have fun with stars by making and eating their very own. Before class, bake star-shaped cookies.

Materials Needed:

one or two cookies per child, small bowls of colored icing, variety of edible decorations, waxed paper, plastic knives

Directions:

Pass out sheets of waxed paper, plastic knives, icing, edible decorations, and prebaked cookies to the children. Allow the children to "create" their own star masterpieces. For fun and originality, encourage them to name their stars. Read Job 38:31–32 to help the children learn some names God gave the stars.

For More Fun

The children can cut out stars from various colors of paper, decorate them, write a name on each, and hang them as mobiles using hangers.

Sky Lights

Based on Genesis 1:14–19

The finger play below is a fun way for children to remember exactly what God created on the fourth day.

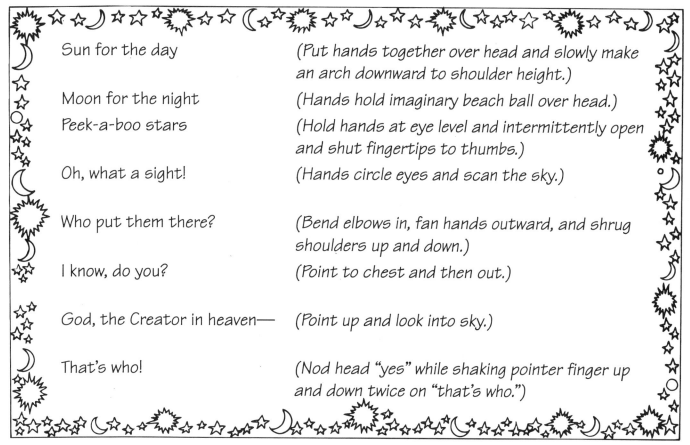

Sun for the day — (Put hands together over head and slowly make an arch downward to shoulder height.)

Moon for the night — (Hands hold imaginary beach ball over head.)

Peek-a-boo stars — (Hold hands at eye level and intermittently open and shut fingertips to thumbs.)

Oh, what a sight! — (Hands circle eyes and scan the sky.)

Who put them there? — (Bend elbows in, fan hands outward, and shrug shoulders up and down.)

I know, do you? — (Point to chest and then out.)

God, the Creator in heaven— — (Point up and look into sky.)

That's who! — (Nod head "yes" while shaking pointer finger up and down twice on "that's who.")

When I play Outside for fun, I thank the Lord For our wonderful sun.

I see the moon In the sky at night. Thank You, God, For this bright light.

Thank You, God, For the stars in the sky, Above all the clouds, Way up high!

Light Fun

Let the children create their very own light poems/pictures to thank God for giving us the sun, moon, and stars.

Materials Needed:

paper, crayons, glue, glitter, markers, scissors

Directions:

Give each child a sheet of paper. Each child can draw, decorate, and cut out a sun, moon, or star. (You could give each child a pre-drawn and copied sun, moon, or star if you prefer.) Help the children write poems about the sun, moon, or stars in the center of their cutouts. (You can write them as a class if the children need help.) Display them on a bulletin board.

God's Great Lights

Based on Genesis 1:14–19

Day 4

God created many things for us. Learn about some of them below by adding or subtracting the number from the letters written below the lines. Use the alphabet line for help. (Example: B + 2 = D, two letters to the right)

A B C D E F G H I J K L M N O P Q R S T U V W X Y Z

God made

____ ____ ____ great lights—
R + 2   X – 1   Q – 2

____ ____ ____ for the ____ ____ ____
M + 2 L + 2 G – 2   C + 1 D – 3 Z – 1

and one for the

____ ____ ____ ____ ____.
L + 2 H + 1 J – 3 F + 2 W – 3

He also made the

____ ____ ____ ____ ____.
T – 1 Q + 3 C – 2 P + 2 N + 5

Now write your own message below by using this code and writing under the blanks. (Use only as many blanks as you need.) Give it to a friend to solve.

Thank You, God, for ____ ____ ____ ____ ____ ____ ____ ____.

Lights in the Sky

Based on Genesis 1:14–19

Day 4 was a big day for creating! God created some wonderful things on this day. To find out what they are, fit the underlined words into the correct boxes. Then at the bottom of the page, fill in the blanks with letters and draw pictures of the three things God made.

And God said, "Let there be lights in the . . . sky . . . let them serve as signs and to give light on the earth." God made two great lights . . . to govern the day and . . . the night . . . (Genesis 1:14–16)

S __ __ __   M __ __ __ __   S __ __ __ __ __

Great Groups of Stars

Based on Genesis 1:14–19

Tell the children that a constellation is a group of bright stars that forms an imaginary picture in the night sky. Then read Job 38:31–32 to the children: *". . . Can you loose the cords of Orion? Can you bring forth the constellations in their seasons . . ."*

Explain to the children that Orion is a constellation that looks like a hunter with a bow and arrow. Let the children create their very own Orion constellations following the directions below.

Materials Needed:

one 4½" x 6" piece of dark blue or black construction paper per child; round toothpicks; scissors; paper clips; white, silver, or yellow crayons; one copy of the constellation pattern below per child

Directions:

1. Lay the pattern on top of the construction paper. Place a paper clip on each edge.

2. Poke the pattern dots using a toothpick. Be careful not to make large holes—just puncture through the paper and stop.

3. Remove the paper clips and pattern.

4. Use a crayon to draw thin, straight lines between the holes, using the pattern as a guide. Use a second color to draw the body as shown. There are no stars for the head or lower legs.

5. Hold the constellation up to the light to view.

6. Mount all of the constellations on a bulletin board with a white background or place them in the windows.

SS48836

Birds and Fish

Based on Genesis 1:20–23

When Kids Ask . . .

Below are some questions the children may ask in regards to the fifth day of creation. Give four children one of the questions to ask, or divide the children into groups and give each group a question. You can use the Bible verses listed to help you answer the questions, or you can let the children come up with their own answers.

1. *Does God care about birds as much as He cares about people?* (Deuteronomy 22:6–7; Matthew 6:26)

2. *Did God create sea monsters?* (Genesis 1:21; Psalm 104:25–26; Job 41)

3. *Did a whale swallow Jonah?* (Jonah 1:17a; Jonah 2:10—It could have been a whale. What is most important is *"the Lord provided,"* or prepared, a special fish which listened to God's voice.)

4. *Does God talk to birds and fish?* (Genesis 1:22—We are told that God talked to the birds and fish, and He blessed them and told them to be fruitful and multiply.)

Fantastic Facts

Below are some fascinating facts relating to birds and fish. Put these on a bulletin board and let the children add to them, illustrate them, or write about them in journals. Or, let groups of children choose one to prepare a report on, create a mural for, find a Bible verse that relates to it, etc.

- In ancient Olympic Games, teams of ostriches (the largest living birds) pulled chariots around a circular track.

- Eagles often use the same nest year after year. One nest measured over 20 feet deep and nearly 10 feet across.

- Hummingbirds are the smallest of all birds. One species can beat its wings 80 times a second.

- A ruby-throated hummingbird can fly up to 500 miles without stopping.

- A crab can bury itself in the sand and still watch what is going on around it. It has two antennae with eyes on the tips which stick up above the sand. It turns them in all directions.

- Though sharks are huge and strong, they are not smart like dolphins. Sometimes dolphins tease sharks by leading them on a game of chase. The sharks swim until they get all tired out. Then the dolphins grin and swim away.

- Some sharks are as large as school buses. Some are as small as your hand.

- The starfish's mouth is in the middle of its body. To eat, the starfish turns its stomach inside out and brings it out through its mouth so it can eat things like clams and oysters.

- The blue whale is earth's largest animal, weighing in at 150 tons—as much as 20 elephants!

Fun Fish Prints

Based on Genesis 1:20–23

These fish prints are a lot of fun for children to make to remind them of what God created on day 5.

Materials Needed:
large and dense vegetables suitable for printing, such as white potatoes, onions, sweet potatoes, turnips (also, celery, carrots, and parsnips make great fish scale designs); assorted colors of tempera paints in shallow tins; paper towels; colored markers; paper; patterns below; cardboard; scissors

Directions:
1. Use the patterns below to make cardboard patterns of the fish. (You may need to reduce them so that they fit.)
2. Cut the vegetables in half.
3. Lay a cardboard fish pattern on one of the vegetable halves. Trace around it with a pencil.
4. Cut away the area outside the pencil line, $1/4$" deep, to form patterns on the vegetables.
5. Dip the vegetables in paint. Blot lightly on a paper towel and then press onto paper.
6. When dry, add scales, fins, etc., using colored markers or celery, parsnip, and carrots.

For More Fun
Let the children make these prints directly on a bulletin board entitled "Fish From God."

What a Bird!

Based on Genesis 1:20–23

"The wings of the ostrich flap joyfully . . ." (Job 39:13)

The ostrich is one of the most interesting birds God created. It is the largest bird. It stands up to 10 feet tall and weighs over 300 pounds. This marvelous bird can run about 30–40 miles per hour for short periods of time. Ostrich eggs weigh over three pounds. How would you like to eat an ostrich egg for breakfast? The female ostrich is grayish brown. The male is black with white on his wings and tail. These large birds like to lay their heads and long necks flat on the ground, but they do not bury their heads in the sand like some people think. Notice the two clawed toes on each foot. The ostrich protects itself by kicking with its feet.

Ostrich feathers are very fluffy and beautiful. People use them for decorations.

Trace the ostrich egg. Use a black crayon to color in the areas on the ostrich that have dots. Use a white crayon to color in the plain areas. Color the legs brownish yellow.

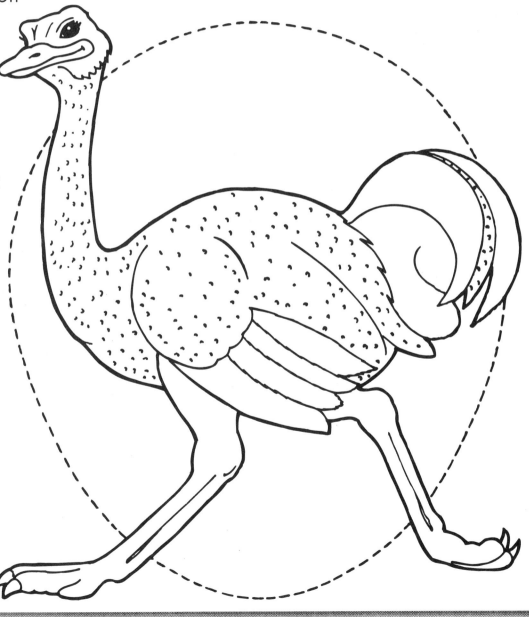

Incredible Creatures

Based on Genesis 1:20–23

. . . "Let the water teem with living creatures, and let birds fly above the earth . . ." (Genesis 1:20)

God created many wonderful and beautiful birds and fish for us to enjoy! Find the bird and fish names in the wordsearch below. All names appear left to right or up and down.

CROW	OWL		CRAB	SEA HORSE
DOVE	ROBIN		EEL	SHARK
EAGLE	SPARROW		JELLYFISH	SHRIMP
LARK	STORK		LOBSTER	TROUT
OSTRICH	WREN		OCTOPUS	WHALE

O	S	T	R	I	C	H	J	S	W	P
J	E	L	L	Y	F	I	S	H	R	W
S	E	A	H	O	R	S	E	R	E	L
P	C	R	O	W	R	O	B	I	N	O
A	H	K	Q	L	E	E	L	M	S	B
R	U	V	E	O	C	T	O	P	U	S
R	J	S	H	A	R	K	H	X	Z	T
O	T	R	O	U	T	E	A	G	L	E
W	H	A	L	E	S	T	O	R	K	R
D	O	V	E	P	N	C	R	A	B	W

Bird Watching in the Bible

Based on Genesis 1:20–23

Some of the many beautiful birds God created are mentioned in the Bible. Use your Bible to look up the references and write the name of each bird mentioned in the blanks.

1. Exodus 19:4 _____

2. Psalm 105:40 _____

3. Genesis 8:7 _____

4. Isaiah 34:15 _____

    and _____

5. Job 39:26 _____

6. Matthew 10:29 _____

7. Zechariah 5:9 _____

8. Genesis 8:8 _____

Draw a picture of your favorite bird.
Fill in the information about it.

name of bird _____

where it lives _____

_____

what it eats _____

_____

interesting _____

fact about it _____

_____

Animals and Man

Based on Genesis 1:24–2:24

When Kids Ask . . .

Below are some questions the children may ask in regards to the sixth day of creation. Give five children one of the questions to ask, or divide the children into groups and give each group a question. You can use the Bible verses listed to help you answer the questions, or you can let the children come up with their own answers.

1. *Will there be animals in heaven?* (Revelation 12:3–4; 13:1–2; 13:11; 17:3—Yes, lots of them. The book of Revelation contains descriptions of unusual animals, unlike any here on earth; Isaiah 11:6–9—The prophet Isaiah tells about the peaceful coexistence of animals and their gentleness with little children in Christ's Kingdom; 1 Corinthians 2:9)

2. *Why did God make man?* (Genesis 1:26; 2:15—The Bible tells us that God made man to care for all the earth, including all of its creatures. This meant man was given responsibility to keep it healthy, productive, and beautiful.)

3. *What is man made of?* (Genesis 2:7; Ecclesiastes 12:7—Unlike any other creature, man was made of the dust of the earth. The body (flesh) is destructible, but the uniqueness of man is that he is created in the image of God with an eternal spirit.)

4. *What is the "image of God?"* (Ecclesiastes 12:7—God is a spirit. He does not have a physical body as we do, but we are made in His likeness with a spirit that lives forever after our body dies; John 4:24—Our spirit communes with God who is a spirit; Genesis 2:7)

5. *Were Adam and Eve created the same way?* (Genesis 2:7—No. Adam was created from the dust; Genesis 2:21–22—Eve was created from Adam's rib bone.)

Fantastic Facts

Below are some fascinating facts relating to animals and man. Put these on a bulletin board and let the children add to them, illustrate them, or write about them in journals. Or, let groups of children choose one to prepare a report on, create a mural for, find a Bible verse that relates to it, etc.

- Spiders never get stuck in their own webs because they weave with two kinds of thread—one is sticky, the other is not. Spiders know to avoid stepping on the sticky thread.

- Not all spiders make webs to catch their dinner. Some make nests like the trap-door spider.

- A mosquito's wings beat 500 times a second.

- The human brain never sleeps.

- A grasshopper can jump 200 times its own length.

- Some elephants in Africa have ears that are 5 feet long.

- A human's outer skin is totally replaced every 15–30 days. It is the largest organ of the body and covers approximately 22 square feet.

- The largest known elephant tusk was 11½ feet long and weighed 236 pounds.

- Over 200 bones make up the human skeleton. The smallest bones are in the ear.

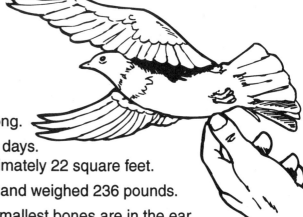

What a Great Day!

Based on Genesis 1:24–2:24

Day 6

What a special day the sixth day of creation was! God made man! He also created the many wonderful animals you love and find fascinating. Read all about the sixth day of creation below. Then fit the underlined words into the numbered spaces in the puzzle.

God made the <u>wild</u> <u>animals</u> according to their <u>kinds</u>, the livestock . . . and all
       14   5   11

the <u>creatures</u> that move along the <u>ground</u> . . . And God <u>saw</u> that it was good.
  7   6   13

. . . "<u>Let</u> us make man in <u>our</u> <u>image</u>, in our <u>likeness</u>, and let them <u>rule</u> over the
  3   9   2   10   8

<u>fish</u> . . . the <u>birds</u> . . . the livestock, over all the <u>earth</u> . . ." (Genesis 1:25–26)
 1   12   4

Animal Riddles

Based on Genesis 1:24–2:24

Read the riddles below to the children and let them try to guess what animals are being described. Then read the Bible passages and discuss with the children how these animals were used by God to accomplish His plans. Talk about the attributes of God in each case.

1. David's son, Absalom, was riding on me. We passed under a big oak tree with low branches. Absalom got hung up in the tree, but I kept on running. What am I? (mule) Read 2 Samuel 18:9. Talk about God's justice.

2. Jesus said it was easier for me to go through the eye of a needle than for a rich man to enter heaven. What am I? (camel) Read Matthew 19:24. Talk about salvation.

3. There was a bunch of us together, and we were hungry. A man of God was thrown into our den for us to eat. But something happened. The powerful Creator sent an angel to close our mouths, and we could not open them at all. What are we? (lions) Read Daniel 6:16–23. Talk about God's protection.

4. My master beat me three times. He did not know I saw the angel of the Lord standing in front of me. The great Creator opened my mouth so I could talk to my master. What am I? (donkey) Read Numbers 22:21–34. Talk about God's anger.

5. I like to steal and kill sheep. Jesus, the Good Shepherd, protects His sheep and won't let me into the sheep pen. What am I? (wolf) Read John 10:7–18. Talk about God's love.

6. I attacked a flock of sheep, but a young shepherd boy grabbed me by my hair. He took the lamb out of my mouth and killed me. What am I? (bear) Read 1 Samuel 17:34–35. Talk about God's strength.

7. Samson rounded up 300 of us and tied our tails together. Then he lit our tails on fire, and we ran through the enemies' fields of grain. What are we? (foxes) Read Judges 15:4–5. Talk about God's vengeance.

8. Jesus commanded evil demons to get out of a man's body and into ours. There were about 2000 of us that ended up drowning in a lake. What are we? (pigs) Read Mark 5:1–13. Talk about God's power over evil.

For More Fun

Let the children create their own riddles about a favorite Bible character. They should each write three clues in the first person, read them to the class, and let the class try to guess who the clues describe. (Example: 1. I was a good man; 2. God told me to build a big boat; 3. I had a floating "zoo." Who am I? Answer—Noah)

Life in the Garden

Based on Genesis 1:24–2:24

Read the children the story below and on page 36 about the creation of man, woman, and animals. Then try some of the activities on page 37.

The man blinked his eyes, then sat up. "Where am I? Who am I?" He looked at his hands and wiggled his fingers. Then he stared at the one kneeling beside him. "Who are you?"

The Master Creator smiled and reached His arm across the man's shoulders. "I am the Lord, your God. I made you from the dust of the earth and breathed my breath into your nostrils. You are Adam, the first man. And this is your home, the Garden of Eden."

Adam stood on his feet and slowly looked around him. His eyes grew wider as he looked at the hundreds of birds and animals circled around him. "Are they Adams, too?"

Again the Great Creator smiled. "No, Adam. These lovely creatures have been created to bring you pleasure and to increase their number and fill all the earth." Just then, a red, green, and blue parrot landed on Adam's shoulder and rubbed its bill against Adam's ear. "It welcomes you, Adam. And your first assignment is to give all these beautiful creatures names. Tomorrow, I will bring you more." Soon Adam was petting cheetahs and lions. Elephants and rhinos followed him as he walked throughout the garden with his Master and Friend.

For days, Adam became familiar with trees and plants and flowers. Every day as the sun was going down, God came into the garden to talk and walk with Adam and to teach him about life.

"You have been tending the garden well, Adam. I see you moved the violets and placed them under the shade trees."

"Yes, Father, and look what I have made here under the palm trees—a special place for us to sit and watch the animals. I tell You, Father, they are a delight to watch. They help one another. They enjoy each other. Look there. See what I mean?"

Life in the Garden continued

Based on Genesis 1:24–2:24

Beyond the trees stood a gigantic giraffe nibbling leaves from an overhanging branch. Climbing up the animal's neck were two raccoons. "Just watch the show, Father. Those little fellows have been climbing up and sliding down the giraffe's neck most of the afternoon." God leaned back and laughed. Then He turned around to a noise behind them. A family of monkeys were jumping between several trees under which a mother leopard was nursing her babies. Just then, a young, mischievous monkey teetered over to the leopard and tried to pick off its spots.

"Ha, ha, ha," laughed Adam, shaking his head in disbelief. "That little monkey thinks those spots will come off as little bugs do."

The two friends talked more, and then God said, "Adam, it is not good that you are alone. You need a helpmate. All these creatures have each other, male and female, but you are alone and incomplete."

God caused Adam to fall into a deep sleep. From Adam's side, God removed a rib bone and formed a female to be the man's special helper. When Adam woke up, he saw what God had made just for him. Adam looked into her eyes. He touched her face and held her hands in his and spoke. "I will call you 'Woman,' for you are made of my bones."

The man and the woman tended the garden and cared for the animals which God brought to them. They talked and played with the animals and understood their language. One beautiful and unusual being was the serpent, who enjoyed talking with the woman. One day, the serpent slowly slithered his sleek body closer to the woman and looked into her face with penetrating, appealing eyes. "I'll be back tomorrow," he said, "and I'll tell you more about that tree in the middle of the garden."

The woman took a step backward, then agreed, nodding her head. "I'll look forward to your visit." She turned and walked back to join Adam who was standing under a tree, watching its blossoms gently moving in the late afternoon breeze.

"Oh Adam, our garden home is so beautiful! I love everything in it."

"I know. I do, too," answered Adam. "Here comes Father Creator to walk and talk. Let's tell Him how much we love Him, too."

THE END

Life in the Garden continued

Based on Genesis 1:24–2:24

Day 6

Questions for Discussion

1. Adam and God were special friends. How is God your special friend?

2. God gave Adam and Eve many gifts. What are some gifts God has given you?

3. God created so many wonderful animals. What are your favorite animals?

4. The serpent said he would be back tomorrow. What did the serpent trick Eve into doing?

5. Eventually, Adam and Eve disobeyed God. What can you do to show God you are sorry when you disobey Him?

Things to Do

- Let the children illustrate the story. Groups of children could illustrate different parts of the story.

- The children could create a Garden of Eden mural. Let them add texture to it with three-dimensional leaves, tails, etc. Provide children with mural paper, construction paper, fabric scraps, sequins, yarn, string, markers, buttons, glue, etc.

- Help the children create "Sixth Day of Creation" mini books, featuring the things God created on the sixth day.

- The children could create "Sixth Day of Creation Collages." Have them cut out and glue pictures in collage fashion depicting what God created on the sixth day.

- Let the children plant flowers or other plants to create their very own gardens.

- The children could create animal posters. Let each child choose an animal, draw it, and write facts about it on posterboard. Display them around the room.

- Divide the children into groups. Assign each group a set of animals (examples, jungle animals, forest animals, sea animals, furry animals, reptiles, mammals, etc.). The groups can prepare reports and include murals of their assigned sets of animals. Each group can present its report to the class.

GOD CREATED...
FROGS

FROG FACTS:

Let's Get Some Rest!

Based on Genesis 2:2–3

By the seventh day God had finished the work he had been doing; so on the seventh day he rested from all his work. And God blessed the seventh day and made it _____, because on it he rested from all the work of creating that he had done. (Genesis 2:2–3)

Follow the directions below to color the squares in each row of the puzzle grid as directed. This will help you find the word that belongs in the blank above.

	A	B	C	D	E	F	G	H	I	J	K	L	M	N	O
1															
2															
3															
4															
5															

Row 1:   A-C-E-F-G-I-K-O

Row 2:   A-C-E-G-I-L-N

Row 3:   A-B-C-E-G-I-M

Row 4:   A-C-E-G-I-M

Row 5:   A-C-E-F-G-I-J-K-M

God says, *"Remember the Sabbath day by keeping it holy."* (Exodus 20:8) Write three activities you can do that are holy.

_____

_____

_____

What Did God Do?

Based on Genesis 1–2:3

Can you remember what God did each day? Find out by reading each sentence below. Then write the numbers 1–7 in the boxes to show the correct order.

God . . .   **on day . . .**

made fish and birds   ☐

made sky and waters   ☐

made animals and man   ☐

made day and night   ☐

made land, seas, plants, and trees   ☐

rested   ☐

made the sun, moon, and stars   ☐

Draw a picture of something God created that you like very much. Write on what day God created it.

God created _____ on day _____.

"Celebrate Creation" Pennants

These seven pennants are a great way to decorate a number of areas to remind the children and others of the many wonderful things God created. Each child can create his or her own set of pennants, or groups of children can work on a set. Make one each day, or each week. The size of pennants is relative to their intended purpose as well as the quantity and availability of materials. Places for displaying pennants may include 1) above a classroom chalkboard; 2) in a hallway outside the classroom; 3) in the church vestibule; 4) in the fellowship hall; 5) suspended from a clothesline and used during a children's presentation.

Materials Needed:

felt (paper will work) in these colors: black, white, light blue, medium blue, gray, orange, green, brown, red, yellow, lavender, aqua, pink, off-white; patterns below and on pages 41–43; white glue; fabric paints; scissors

Directions:

1. Pre-determine the desired size of the pennants.

2. Below and on pages 41–43 are directions and patterns for each of the seven pennants. Enlarge any patterns, if necessary.

3. For continuity, make a sturdy pennant pattern the size of a completed pennant and use this when beginning each pennant.

4. Lay the pennant pattern on the background color of felt and cut out. Be aware that not all pennants are constructed of one background color. Piecing of colors is sometimes necessary.

5. Pin the patterns from pages 42–43 to felt and cut out.

6. Use white glue to bond the felt pieces together.

7. Decorate the patterns and pennants with fabric paints as directed.

8. Glue "DAY" and "Number" to the bottom of each pennant.

9. If desired, affix cloth or paper trim to pennant edges in your choice of color.

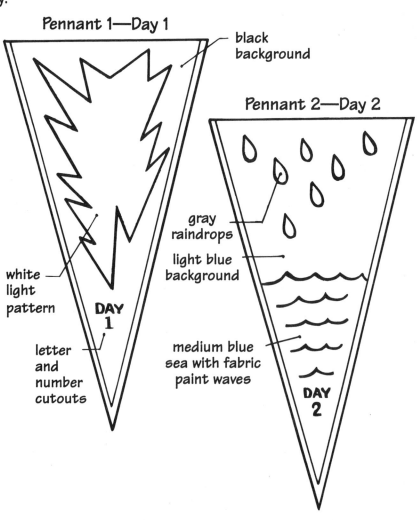

Pennant 1—Day 1

black background

white light pattern

letter and number cutouts

DAY 1

Pennant 2—Day 2

gray raindrops

light blue background

medium blue sea with fabric paint waves

DAY 2

"Celebrate . . ." continued

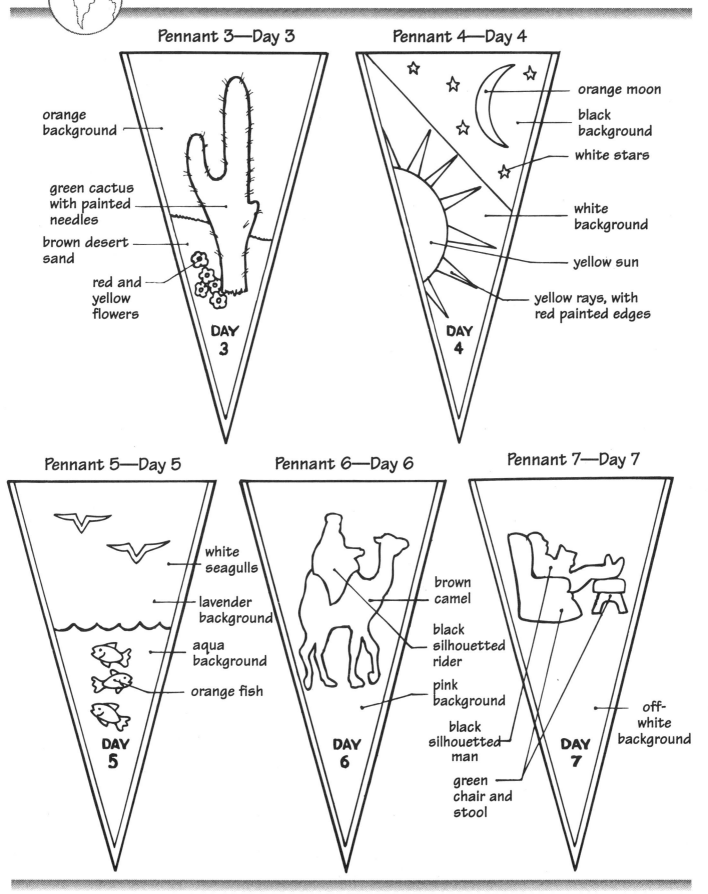

Pennant 3—Day 3

orange background

green cactus with painted needles

brown desert sand

red and yellow flowers

DAY 3

Pennant 4—Day 4

orange moon

black background

white stars

white background

yellow sun

yellow rays, with red painted edges

DAY 4

Pennant 5—Day 5

white seagulls

lavender background

aqua background

orange fish

DAY 5

Pennant 6—Day 6

brown camel

black silhouetted rider

pink background

black silhouetted man

green chair and stool

DAY 6

Pennant 7—Day 7

off-white background

DAY 7

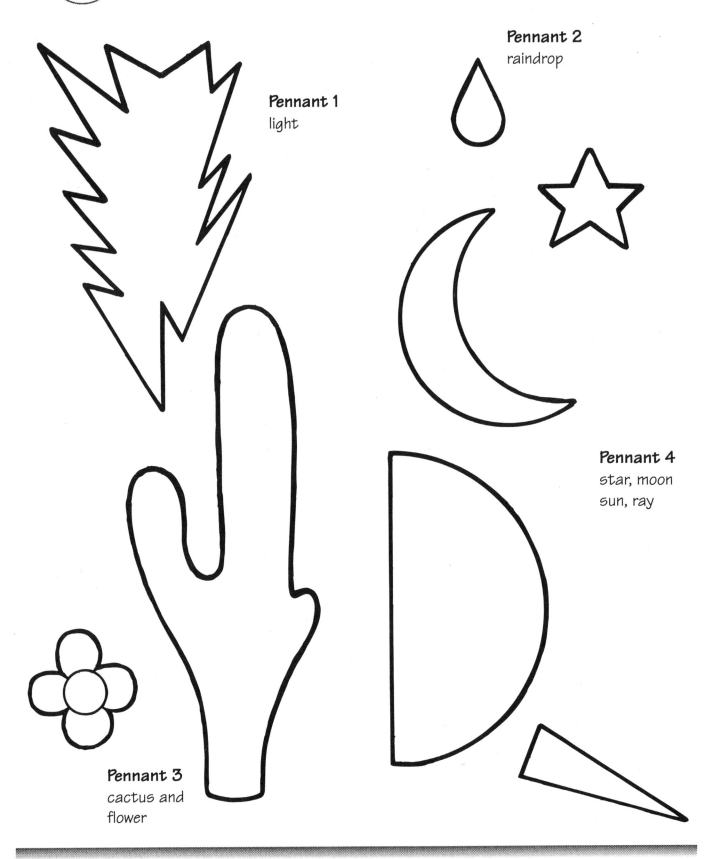

Pennant 1
light

Pennant 2
raindrop

Pennant 4
star, moon
sun, ray

Pennant 3
cactus and
flower

"Celebrate . . ." continued

Pennant 5
fish, seagull

Pennant 6
camel, rider

Pennant 7 chair, stool, man resting

DAY 123
4567

Enlarge and cut numbers and letters out of your choice of color. Glue to bottom of pennant.

SS48836

Celebrate Life!

Below and on page 45 are some great ideas you can use to have a party celebrating God's beautiful creation!

Overhead Decorations

Concentrate on the area above a table. Cut star, sun, and moon shapes from fluorescent posterboard and hang from fish line. Glue cotton batting to front and back of white construction paper clouds and hang from fish line. Cut lightning shapes from fluorescent yellow posterboard. Hang different sizes of Styrofoam™ balls covered with colored foil to simulate the earth, sun, moon, and planets. From 8" circles of gaudy wallpaper, cut spirals to dangle from the ceiling. Fill in spaces with white and blue balloons.

Table Decorations

Cover a table with blue or white paper. Scatter confetti, sequins, and glitter-covered gold and silver stars. Use stickers of animals, plants, or flowers to decorate solid-colored napkins, plates, and cups. These may be personalized with the children's names.

Centerpiece

Decorate the sides of a shallow cardboard box with a scenery of mountains, lakes, and trees. Attach a 2" strip around the bottom which reads *So the man gave names to all the livestock, the birds of the air and all the beasts of the field . . .* (Genesis 1:20) Place individually wrapped gifts (animal erasers, animal pencil tops, plastic birds, fish, insects, etc.) inside the box. Number each gift. After games and refreshments, permit children to draw numbers and receive corresponding numbered party favors.

Special Prize

Have a bowl with four goldfish near the center of the table to be given as a prize for the winner of the Treasure Hunt game (see page 45).

Refreshments

Serve star cookies (see page 22), Jell-O™ jigglers, ice cream, and punch made from 7-Up™ and orange juice.

Celebrate Life! continued

Games

1. **Animal Charades:** Children can imitate the posture and movements of animals, using no sounds.

2. **Over-Under Relay:** Divide children into two lines. Pass a stuffed animal over heads, through legs, etc., up the line and back again. Give the winning team animal crackers.

3. **Unscramble:** (teacher-prepared pencil game) Scramble body-part words (for example, mra = arm, deha = head, etc.). Possible words include eye, ear, hand, knee, nose, cheek, elbow, wrist, heel, toe, neck, back, chest, heart, thumb, leg, foot. Give the children five minutes to unscramble the words.

4. **Feed Willy:** Divide the children into two teams. Prepare two "elephant boxes." (See pattern below.) Give 50 unshelled peanuts to each team. The children use plastic straws to suck up the peanuts and drop them in the "elephant boxes." The winning team gets double the amount of peanuts to eat.

5. **Memory "20" Game:** Place 20 common objects on a table. Give the children two minutes to memorize the objects. Cover the objects with a towel or remove them from sight. Children write the objects they remember on sheets of paper, each containing the numbers 1–20.

Enlarge pattern to fit end of shoebox.

6. **Guessing Game:** Display a large rock. Have children guess the weight. Permit them to lift it. Weigh the rock on a scale. Reward the winner with a painted rock.

7. **Treasure Hunt:** Hide orange paper goldfish all over the room before the party. Provide each child with a plastic bag for the hunt. Give the children three minutes to try to find as many goldfish as possible. Give live goldfish to the winner. Have a second bowl with water ready and divide fish if there is more than one winner. The other children can receive goldfish crackers.

Creation Acrostic

Use the letters in *creation* to write an acrostic poem. Include things God created or try to say "Thank You" to Him for all He has given us. Color the border after you have written your poem.

Creation
Reminds us of God's
Eternal love for
All of us.
Thank You, Father.
I love all of Your gifts.
Only You have the power to create.
No one is greater than You.

Cats and dogs
Rabbits and horses
Elephants and giraffes
Alligators and fish
Tigers and lions
Iguanas and lizards
Octopuses and sea horses
Never forget to say, "Thank You, God!"

C
R
E
A
T
I
O
N

SS48836

What a Busy Seven Days!

Label seven sheets of paper 1–7, one page per day of creation. Color and cut out the pictures below. Glue them to the correct sheet of paper. There is nothing to glue on day 1 or 7. Draw your own pictures for these days. Add more pictures or words to the pages if you like. Assemble the pages in order. Make a cover page and staple the pages together. Share your Creation Book with a friend.

SS48836

Answer Key

Page 6

waters

Page 9

N		A		P		G		Y	
	(E)		(M)	O		(T)		S	
T		(A)	(T)		R		H		
	(W)		(E)		R	(E)		(R)	
F		(I)	T		(H)		K		
	(L)		P	(G)		(S)		(T)	
(E)		N	M		(T)		Y		
	R		(A)	(R)		M		(H)	
W			(G)		S		(T)		
	(N)	(I)		E		(H)		R	

1. EMPTY   2. WATER
3. LIGHT   4. EARTH
5. NIGHT

Page 11

Pictures are in order going across.

1, 2, 3
4, 5, 6

Page 13

F	D	U	O	L	C	E	S	R	A	I	N
R	M	R	O	T	S	A	L	E	R	N	B
O	D	R	O	P	K	R	E	T	I	H	W
Z	L	I	A	H	Y	T	E	A	A	B	Z
E	W	O	N	S	Y	H	T	W	I	N	D
N	D	E	W	E	Q	L	W	O	D	H	F

Page 14

Possible answers:
5. rain, snow, hail, etc.
6. ponds, lakes, seas, puddles, streams, etc.

Page 16

S	O	U	T	H	A	M	E	R	I	C	A
E	U	R	O	P	E	A	F	R	I	C	A
A	N	T	A	R	C	T	I	C	A	S	I	A
N	O	R	T	H	A	M	E	R	I	C	A
		A	U	S	T	R	A	L	I	A	

Page 18

Page 24

two, one, day, night, stars

Page 25

sun, moon, stars

Page 30

O	S	T	R	I	C	H	J	S	W	P
J	E	L	L	Y	F	I	S	H	R	W
S	E	A	H	O	R	S	E	R	E	L
P	C	R	O	W	R	O	B	I	N	O
A	H	K	Q	L	E	E	L	M	S	B
R	U	V	E	O	C	T	O	P	U	S
R	J	S	H	A	R	K	H	X	Z	T
O	T	R	O	U	T	E	A	G	L	E
W	H	A	L	E	S	T	O	R	K	R
D	O	V	E	P	N	C	R	A	B	W

Page 31

1. eagle
2. quail
3. raven
4. owl and falcon
5. hawk
6. sparrow
7. stork
8. dove

Page 33

Page 38

Page 39

5, 2, 6, 1, 3, 7, 4